RELEASED FROM CIRCULATION

WAYNE-WE

D0893978

WAYNE-WESTLAND
PUBLIC LIBRARY
35000 SIMS AVE.
WAYNE, MI. 48184
721-7832

J
BIOG
ROB INSO

WAYNE-WESTLAND
PUBLIC LIBRARY
35000 SIMS AVE.
WAYNE, MI. 48184
721-7832

Aaseng, Nathan.
    Sports great David Robinson / Nathan
Aaseng. -- Hillside, N.J. : Enslow
Publishers, c1992.

    64 p. : ill. ; pc 4 and up. -- (Sports
great books)
                          59130   NOV '92
    SUMMARY: Discusses the career of the San
Antonio Spurs team member who also played-
basketball for the United States Naval
Academy and the American Olympic team.
    ISBN 0-89490-373-X(lib.bdg.) : $15.95

    1. Robinson, David, 1965-   2.
Afro-Americans--Biography.   I. Title.   II.
Series.

                                             23

                                   91-41532 /AC

SPORTS GREAT DAVID ROBINSON

—Sports Great Books—

SPORTS GREAT DAVID ROBINSON

Nathan Aaseng

—Sports Great Books—

Enslow Publishers, Inc.

Bloy St.& Ramsey Ave.	P.O. Box 38
Box 777	Aldershot
Hillside, N.J. 07205	Hants GU12 6BP
U.S.A.	U.K.

WAYNE – WESTLAND
PUBLIC LIBRARY
35000 SIMS AVE.
WAYNE, MI. 48184
721-7832

Copyright ©1992 by Nathan Aaseng

All rights reserved.

No part of this book may be reproduced by any means without the written permission of the publisher.

Library of Congress Cataloging-in-Publication Data

Aaseng, Nathan.
   Sports great David Robinson / Nathan Aaseng.
      p. cm. — (Sports great books)
   Includes index.
   Summary: Discusses the life and career of the San Antonio Spurs team member whose background includes playing basketball for the United States Naval Academy and the American Olympic team.
   ISBN 0-89490-373-X
   1. Robinson, David, 1965–   —Juvenile literature. 2. Basketball players—United States—Juvenile literature. 3. San Antonio Spurs (Basketball team)—literature. [1. Robinson, David, 1965–   . 2. Basketball players. 3. Afro-Americans—Biography.] I. Title. II. Series.
GV884.R615A615 1992
796.323'092—dc20
[B]
                                                           91-41532
                                                              CIP
                                                              AC

3 9082 06451674 6

Printed in the United States of America

10 9 8 7 6 5 4 3 2 1

Photo Credits: NBA/Andrew D. Bernstein, p. 50; NBA/Barry Gossage, pp. 11, 34, 37, 41, 42, 56, 57, 59; NBA/Betsy Peabody Rowe,7 pp. 8, 48; NBA/John Soohoo, p. 55; San Antonio Spurs, pp. 6, 44, 46; University of Pittsburgh, p. 23; U.S. Department of Defense, D.E. Erickson, p. 15; U.S. Navy, pp. 20, 30.

Cover Photo: NBA/Andrew D. Bernstein

Contents

David Robinson

Chapter 1

As the time clock wound down to 90 seconds, two huge basketball players in the center of the lane got so tangled they looked like one giant octopus. David Robinson and Patrick Ewing—two of the top centers in the National Basketball Association (NBA)—leaned, shoved, and jostled for position.

San Antonio's Robinson broke free, caught a pass, and floated high into the air. His soft jumper dropped through the net to add to his team's narrow lead. New York tried to answer by going to their star, Ewing. But Robinson cut around Ewing and stole the pass to start a fast break. Next, Ewing tried to score on a drive, but this time Robinson swatted the ball away, and San Antonio hung on to win 101–97.

Performances such as this one make David Robinson a coach's dream. If coaches could order the perfect center from a factory, they could hardly do better than the San Antonio star.

David Robinson stands 7 feet 1 inch, can dribble as well as a small guard, and can walk across a gymnasium floor on his hands. With his trim body (his waist is only 33 inches around)

Most big men cannot dribble as well as the smaller guards, but Robinson is not afraid to put the ball on the floor.

and lean legs, he can sprint downcourt faster than any 7-footer who ever played the game. Yet his upper body is packed with muscles that an arm wrestling champion would envy. This strength helps him hold his own in the rugged turf wars for rebounding position.

Robinson may be the most intelligent athlete ever to step on to an NBA court. One of his pro coaches, Larry Brown, has said that Robinson "accepts coaching as well as anyone I've seen." Robinson is easy to be around. He is also polite and respectful—almost to a fault. And, for good measure, he has that soft, accurate jump shot. David Robinson's speed and coordination allow him to do things no other big man can do. Other pro centers have been able to soar high to block a shot or snatch the ball out of the air, and fire a pass to a guard in the open court. But Robinson can also catch up to the action, take the pass, and finish the fast break with a monster slam dunk—all before the defense can get set!

Veteran NBA coach Cotton Fitzsimmons has called Robinson "the greatest impact player the league has seen since Kareem Abdul-Jabbar." Others say that Robinson reminds them of Bill Russell—the most intimidating center who ever played basketball. The main differences are that Robinson is taller, faster, and a better athlete than Russell was in his playing years.

Then again, this dream player can be a basketball coach's nightmare. Few pro athletes have made it as far as Robinson has with so little interest in their sport. Robinson reluctantly played just one year of basketball before entering college. He knew so little about the game that his coach at the United States Naval Academy felt as though he were working with a freshman in high school.

Although he rapidly became the best college player in the country, Robinson insisted that basketball was just something he did for fun. He shook his head in disbelief at teammates who would actually work on their game after practice had ended. He always had other interests that were at least as important as basketball. Robinson enjoyed playing the piano or solving an advanced mathematical problem.

For sports fanatics who think athletes should eat, sleep, and breath their sport, Robinson's approach to the game is like hearing fingernails scratch a chalkboard. One coach after another has felt he was beating his head against a wall trying to get Robinson to make the sport the most important thing in his life. The more they screamed at him, the less he cared about the game.

Sometimes Robinson's mind even wanders when he is trying to pay attention. Every so often he drifts off in his own world and forgets about basketball, even in the middle of a game. Coach Brown just sighs, "I don't know where David goes when he loses his concentration."

As if all that were not enough to drive a coach out of the business, Robinson is always asking questions. His active mind needs to pick apart problems to get at the logical solution. That does not fit with the coaching style of many successful coaches who expect their instructions to be followed without question. They feel it is hard for them to hold onto their control of a team with someone like Robinson interrupting to ask why they are doing certain things.

When Robinson showed up for the Spurs training camp in San Antonio in 1989, basketball experts were not certain what to expect. Robinson's duties in the Navy had taken him away from basketball for two years. How much had the long layoff hurt him?

Just before training camp, Robinson's performance as center for the U. S. Olympic team had been disappointing. Was that performance a true sign of his ability? Or could he really be as good as some scouts had thought when they had watched him in college?

The Spurs' rookie seemed as determined as ever to open his mind to new subjects and challenges outside of basketball. Could Robinson, a person with so many outside interests, devote himself to learning how to play basketball? Or would he get bored with the game? What was in store for his NBA coaches: A coach's dream or a nightmare?

Coaches and fans alike wondered what was in store for Robinson as a pro.

Chapter 2

Ambrose Robinson knew how it felt to perform under pressure. As a high school student in Little Rock, Arkansas, Robinson had scored well on a college entrance exam. The achievement should have been a proud moment for him. But in that time of racial unrest, his score drew only anger and suspicion. Test officials refused to believe that Robinson, who was black, could score so much higher than most of the white students. The officials accused him of cheating.

Robinson was forced to retake the test under the hostile glare of test officials. Any slipup on his part would be considered proof that he had cheated. Ambrose Robinson met the challenge. He scored even higher the second time than he had the first! His success on the test opened the way to a distinguished career as a submarine sonar technician in the U.S. Navy.

Ambrose and his wife, Freda, were stationed in Key West, Florida, when their second child arrived. David Maurice Robinson was born on August 6, 1965. David inherited a great deal of his father's brilliance—and then some.

The Robinsons moved to Virginia Beach, Virginia, shortly after David's birth. There, David showed an amazing ability to learn. As soon as he entered first grade, he was placed in a special program for gifted children. One of his favorite games as a small child was to add up his mother's grocery bill in his head before the cart was unloaded at the checkout line!

Ambrose Robinson was a demanding teacher, himself. He insisted that his young son read through the entire dictionary to improve his vocabulary. In junior high, when David came home with an *A*, two *B*s, and a *C* on his a report card, his dad grounded him for six weeks.

Ambrose, however, was not a competitive man. When principals suggested that David be moved up a grade in school, Ambrose said no. Rather than pushing David to excel at any one thing, he kept encouraging his son to try new things.

Ambrose taught David a few basic notes on the piano. Then, without a formal lesson, David learned to play classical music by ear.

Ambrose also taught him basic electronics. When the elder Robinson was shipped out to sea before putting together a widescreen television he had bought, 12-year-old David assembled it on his own. The boy even figured out how to solder the connections without having ever soldered before. At the age of 14, David enrolled in an advanced computer course.

David not only developed the same wide-ranging curiosity as his Dad, he also picked up his father's relaxed attitude and wandering attention span. However, Freda Robinson was not about to let her son coast along, dabbling in whatever caught his fancy. She encouraged him to set goals and accomplish something with his talents.

Ambrose Robinson was often sent out to sea aboard ships. He could be away from home for as long as six months at a time. Freda also worked full time as a nurse. The Robinsons' busy work schedules forced their children to accept a great deal of responsibility. David, his older sister Kim, and younger brother Chuck often cooked their own meals, did the housework, and completed their homework without being nagged.

Despite the absences of Ambrose and Freda and the extra work, the Robinson household was exceptionally calm and stress-free. "I had responsibility, but I had freedom too,"

The submarine piers at Norfolk, Virginia, where Ambrose Robinson was stationed.

Robinson says. "So I never had a desire to break loose." The family was very close, and the only hero David ever had was his dad. David's dream was to follow his father into the Navy. He planned a career in science.

Although he did not follow sports closely, and was not very good at them, David went out for a half dozen sports as a youth. However, he considered sports to be nothing more than one of life's many curiosities. In some ways he did not fit in with other boys. He took what people said so literally that most jokes went over his head. Sports were not as easy for him as most things that he attempted, and so he did not develop much confidence in his athletic skill. He tried out for basketball during his freshman year of high school and found himself sitting on the bench. When David thought his coach was going to cut him from the team, he quit. David also had difficulty focusing on the many routine drills that are a part of all sports learning. Robinson dropped out of track in high school because it was too boring, switching instead to baseball.

One of his best sports was gymnastics. But gymnastics is not a sport for large people. Robinson, who stood only 5 feet 5 inches when he was 14, began to grow. By his senior year he had sprouted to 6 feet 7 inches. That was too much body to whirl around in gymnastics.

At the beginning of David's senior year, his father retired from the Navy. The family moved off-base to Woodbridge, Virginia—just outside Washington, D.C. When David Robinson showed up for classes at Osbourne Park High School in Manassas, Virginia, the basketball players were excited. They looked at this tall newcomer and hoped he could put his height to use on their team.

But Robinson was not interested in trying basketball again. He sometimes played a game of basketball with friends, but he did not really enjoy it. "The game didn't come naturally to me," Robinson said. "I had no particular gift for it. I was just a tall kid." He was also well aware of how little he knew about the fine points of the game that most high school players had learned years before. In the end, however, Robinson finally gave into the pressure and went out for the team.

Robinson displayed surprising coordination while playing for Osbourne Park. But he found basketball to be more work than fun. To take advantage of his height, Robinson was placed near the basket. In this position, he was knocked around by stronger, more aggressive players. Robinson's coach could tell the kid's heart was not really into this kind of action. He worried that his center might lose all interest. There were, in fact, many times when Robinson could hardly wait for the season to end. He said, "I just wanted to stick it out so I could get my letter." Robinson did stick it out. In fact, he played so well that he was voted his team's most valuable player and was named to the All-Metro second team. The honors were all very interesting and a little surprising to David. But they did not mean much to him. Far more important to him was the spectacular score he achieved on his college entrance exams in his senior year. That cleared the way for Robinson to attend the United States Naval Academy in Annapolis, Maryland, in the fall of 1983.

Had Robinson started his growth spurt any earlier than he did, he would have been turned down by the Navy. Because of the limited space built into Navy ships and airplanes, the Naval Academy does not accept very tall applicants. Entrants must be 6 feet 6 inches or under, with a few exceptions made for persons up to 6 feet 8 inches.

Robinson's father Ambrose, at 6 feet 6 inches, had barely slipped under the limit. And David himself squeezed in by a hair's width. At the time he entered the academy he was bumping the 6 feet, 8 inch cutoff. Fortunately for Robinson, once people are accepted into the academy, they can remain even if they grow past the limit. Within weeks after entering the academy, Robinson shot past the upper height limit. To everyone's surprise he was not nearly finished growing.

Chapter 3

Not every young adult can thrive under the discipline of a military academy. Life at the academy is strictly controlled by rules. Freedoms that many college students take for granted, such as keeping radios in the bedroom and running out for a bite of fast food late at night, are taken away.

Yet Robinson enjoyed life at the academy. His logical, probing mind loved the structure and order of his schedule. He dove into the mental challenges of advanced calculus, computer science, and physics. Some of the more difficult Navy requirements helped him learn a few things about himself. For example, Robinson despaired when he heard of the Navy drill that required him to swim for 30 minutes without stopping. He discovered, to his surprise, that he could do it. That experience led him to have more confidence in himself.

Navy also had a basketball team—as if that really mattered to Robinson. Although still not especially fond of the game, Robinson agreed to build on the surprising success he had found at Osbourne Park.

Basketball had always been a low-key sport at Navy. The academy's height restrictions worked against it. Navy's basketball players were usually shorter than their opponents, especially at the center position. Also Naval Academy graduates were required to serve fulltime in the Navy for five years after graduation. Any high school player basketball players talented enough to consider playing pro ball would have been crazy to go to Navy. As a result, Navy had not had an All-American in basketball since Elliott Loughlin played in 1933. They had not even qualified for the National Collegiate Athletic Association post-season tournament since 1966.

Navy Coach Paul Evans could hardly believe his good fortune when this graceful, 6-foot 9-inch athlete walked onto

Robinson studies computer printout data at the United States Naval Academy.

the court. Robinson was already the tallest player in Navy history—and he was still growing. Yet he was coordinated enough to earn an A in gymnastics at the academy.

Evans' surprise turned to amazement when he discovered how little Robinson actually knew about basketball. Evans tried to look on the bright side of this inexperience. Robinson had picked up "no bad habits from the playground," he said. "It's like teaching a ninth grader who wants to learn."

Before long, however, Evans began to doubt whether Robinson did want to learn. The freshman just did not seem that interested in the game. As one assistant coach admitted, "He's not exactly a coach's player."

Robinson's progress was halted before he had a chance to show his coaches what he could do in his first year. During a boxing class Robinson injured his hand so badly that he had to sit out the first four games of the basketball season. When David finally got into a game, he barely touched the ball. Robinson's first-game numbers read: "0 points, 1 rebound."

Robinson did not crack into the starting lineup all season. The basketball squad was one of the best to play at Navy in many years. It earned the first 20-win season in Navy's history with only modest help from Robinson. When he did play Robinson shot poorly from the free throw line. And with only 195 pounds on his 6-foot 9-inch frame, he took his lumps from older, more muscular opponents. But he improved steadily. Robinson finished the 1983–84 season averaging 7.6 points, 4.0 rebounds, and 1.3 blocked shots per game. Ordinary as those statistics seem, they were not bad for a beginning, and were enough for Robinson to earn his conference's Rookie of the Year award.

This taste of big-time college competition aroused Robinson's interest in basketball. During the summer of 1984 he played against tough competition in the Washington Urban

Coalition League. Robinson lifted weights with a vengeance, adding 20 pounds of muscle—mostly to his upper body. He also continued to grow. When he reported for practice in his sophomore season at 6 feet 11 inches, he towered over his teammates. Robinson's new size and strength alone were enough to earn him the starting spot at center. He opened the season by outplaying some smaller opponents. While observers were impressed, they wondered what would happen when Robinson was matched up against a capable big man.

They found out in December of 1984 when Navy traveled to the Midwest to play in a tournament. Two of their opponents, Southern Illinois and Western Illinois, had strong pivot players. The Navy sophomore center dominated the tournament with 68 points and 31 rebounds. For basketball fans throughout the country who had never heard of Robinson, it was an eye-opening performance. The performance also opened Robinson's eyes. For the first time he began to realize how good he could be at this game.

If Coach Evans thought Robinson would now dedicate his life to the game, however, he was wrong. Evans once visited Robinson at his home to talk to him about basketball. According to the coach, Robinson "spent the whole time showing me a television he had put together." During practice he worked hard but continued to show little enthusiasm for the game. Teammates invited him to join them for extra workouts at the gym. Robinson could not believe they were serious. He had far too many things to do to bother spending any time practicing on his own. "Basketball is just something else to do," he told his dad.

Yet he finished the 1984–85 season with an average of 23.6 points, 11.6 rebounds, and 4.0 blocks per game. Thanks to Robinson, Navy earned its first trip to the NCAA championships in more than a quarter century. In three short

Like many of Robinson's basketball coaches, Navy coach Paul Evans was puzzled as to how to handle his reluctant star center

years, despite treating the game as merely something to fill his spare time, Robinson had become a college star. In fact, pro scouts who had never heard of Robinson a year before were now calling him one of the best "big man" prospects in the college ranks.

As Robinson began to realize how easily he could dominate a basketball game, he had to rethink his future. Suppose he really was good enough to be a pro star? Once Midshipmen, as Navy undergraduates are called, entered their junior year at the academy, there were committed to five years of service after graduation. Some experts, such as Washington Bullet general manager Bob Ferry thought that something could be worked out even if Robinson stayed in the Navy. "Robinson is so good, I'd take him on weekends," Ferry said.

But most agreed that the five-year hitch would badly hurt, and probably ruin, any chance of a pro career. By staying at Navy, Robinson could be throwing away millions of dollars. Reluctantly he had to consider abandoning ship at the Naval Academy.

"Basically, I was scared," Robinson said later. "Would I be comfortable anywhere else?" Navy was where he felt most at home, where he had always wanted to be. In the end Robinson put loyalty to the Navy and to his other interests over a basketball career.

Robinson was praised for not letting the almighty dollar rule his life, for choosing to serve his country instead of his own self-interest. But even though he did make a sacrifice to stay, Robinson denied that he was quite the saint that many thought he was. He later said, "You can assume that if they had shown inflexibility or heartlessness, I would have walked the other way." In fact, there had been a number of meetings between Robinson and U.S. Navy officials to work out a solution to his awkward situation. The Navy desperately wanted to keep Robinson. Not only did he give a good impression of the Navy with his basketball play, but he was a well-mannered, clean-cut, intelligent spokesman. David Robinson was a walking, slam-dunking advertisement for recruiting young people to join the Navy.

There were even better grounds for making exceptions in Robinson's case. His late growth spurt had pushed him to near 7 feet. A man his size simply could not perform active duty on either a ship or an airplane. Through no fault of his own, Robinson's value to the Navy as anything other than a spokesman and role model was limited. In view of all this Robinson and the Navy agreed to share the sacrifice. It was privately understood that Robinson's five-year active duty obligation would be reduced to two years.

Chapter 4

Now that Robinson had his sights on an NBA career, Coach Evans expected his junior center would have no trouble focusing his attention on the game. For Robinson, though, there was always far more to life than just basketball. Evans' dream player turned into a coach's nightmare. The coach grew frustrated with his star's practice habits. He found it hard to believe that a player as good as Robinson was playing the game just for enjoyment, and was not that concerned with wins and statistics. Evans tried to motivate Robinson by screaming at him. During one practice, he threw the center out of the gym for lack of effort.

Such tactics may work with some players, but were exactly the wrong thing to do with Robinson. For Robinson problems are solved by analyzing the situation and discovering the solution. He was not used to being yelled at, and it only made him angry at his coach. Communication between Evans and Robinson worsened.

The friction hardly seemed necessary. Even if Robinson spent his time playing piano or building electronic equipment or working out mathematical brain teasers, he was still the best center in college basketball. He scored 33 points and grabbed 20 rebounds against George Mason College. Robinson swatted away 14 shot attempts against the University of North Carolina-Wilmington, an NCAA record. He scored 37 points against Delaware, and pulled down 25 rebounds in a game against Fairfield University.

For the 1985–86 season, the Navy center averaged 22.7 points and 13.0 rebounds per game. But the statistic that really caught the scouts' eyes was his 207 blocked shots (5.9 per game). That shattered the all-time college record. In fact, only one team, national champion University of Louisville, blocked as many shots that year as Robinson did by himself!

Not everyone was impressed by Robinson's numbers, however. The Fairfields and George Masons were not exactly college powerhouses. Navy played a fairly weak schedule, and not everyone was convinced that Robinson could handle tough competition.

The big test came in the spring of 1986 when Navy was again invited to the NCAA tournament. After defeating the University of Tulsa in their opening game, Navy was matched against powerful Syracuse University. Syracuse's talented front line was far better than anything Robinson had faced before. These players had also been battle-hardened from a season of play against rugged Big East Conference opponents. Instead of backing away from Syracuse's bruising front line, however, Robinson went on the attack. Navy's guards kept feeding the ball inside to Robinson who took it straight to the basket. Although he was fouled repeatedly, Robinson kept banging away. He was awarded 27 foul shots and he sank 21 of them, both Navy records. Led by Robinson's effort, Navy pulled off a shocking upset, 97–85, on Syracuse's home court.

Navy advanced against another giant-killer, Cleveland State University. Although intimidated by 9 Robinson blocks, the Vikings threatened to break the game open late in the second half. Robinson almost single-handedly answered each Cleveland State score. He scored 12 of Navy's final 16 points. This included a shot with six seconds remaining that sealed the victory. The victory put underdog Navy into the final group of eight schools playing for the NCAA championship.

In the quarterfinals, Navy was easily outgunned by a well-balanced Duke University squad. Robinson, the man who had never taken the game seriously before, was stung by the defeat and embarrassed by his team's performance.

When the season was over Robinson joined the U. S. 1986 World Championship team. By this time he had earned so much respect that he was considered the key to the American title hopes. The Soviet Union was favored to win the competition because of their star center, Arvidas Sabonis. Robinson was the only American who had the size and the talent to compare with the 7-foot 2-inch Sabonis. If Robinson could at least slow down Sabonis, the Americans might have a chance.

Robinson played well as the United States advanced to the final round against the Soviet Union. Spurred by the challenge of playing against the best, he came alive in the finals. Robinson outplayed the Soviet star, especially in the crucial closing minutes, as the U. S. team won the championship.

Robinson returned for his senior season in a positive frame of mind. Coach Evans had left to take another job and was replaced by Pete Hermann. Hermann's milder approach to the game suited Robinson perfectly. "He allowed me to be myself, so I worked harder," Robinson said. While he kept up all his other interests, he was all business on the basketball court.

No one had to tell Robinson when he was not doing his

Robinson demonstrates the form that made him the most feared shot blocker in the college game.

job. The towering center burned for a chance to redeem himself after any below average performance. During his senior year Robinson followed up every poor showing with an outstanding game. After scoring only 8 points in a loss to the University of Richmond, Robinson broke loose for 45 points and 21 rebounds against James Madison University. He pounded inside for 43 points and 16 rebounds against a strong Michigan State team after scoring only 13 points against lightly regarded Utica College.

When Navy needed a clutch basket, Robinson was the man to take the shot. His 10-foot turn-around jump shot at the buzzer defeated Michigan State, 91–90. Another turn-around jumper, this time from 17 feet, pulled out a 67–66 win over UNC-Wilmington. With time running out against James Madison, Robinson was forced to throw up a desperation shot from about 40 feet. It banked off the glass and into the net for a 73–71 Navy victory!

Robinson increased his scoring average to 28.2, third best among NCAA players. He ranked fourth in rebounding at 11.8 per game. And his reputation as a shot-blocker scared away many opponents from driving into the lane. As a result his blocked shot total went down, but he still led the nation in that category with 144 (4.5 per game). Robinson was voted the College Player of the Year by nearly every organization making such an award.

Robinson saved his best performances for the toughest teams. On January 25, 1987, Navy traveled to the University of Kentucky to take on the highly ranked Wildcats. Robinson owned the air above the basket that day. On defense he stuffed 10 shots back in the faces of Kentucky shooters and snatched 14 rebounds. On offense he scored 45 of his team's 69 points. Robinson made 17 of 22 shots and sank 11 of 12 free throws for 45 points. Navy lost the game by a score of 80–69, but its center gained new respect that day.

Robinson finished his college career in style. Navy drew the fast-breaking University of Michigan in their first-round contest of the 1987 NCAA tournament. Robinson played his heart out. He hit 22 of 37 shots from the field for a total of 50 points—a new Navy record. But it was not enough as the Wolverines raced to a 97–82 win.

Pro scouts who watched David Robinson soar over the court against Kentucky and Michigan rated him as the best pro prospect of the 1987 draft. Since he was still learning the game, there was a good chance that he could continue to improve. Unfortunately the team that drafted him would have to wait before Robinson could play for them. The big center owed two years of active duty to the Navy before he could play pro ball.

The woeful San Antonio Spurs had first choice in the 1987 draft. The team was so dreadful that it was losing fans as well as money. As badly as they needed quick improvement, the Spurs decided that Robinson was worth the wait. They made him the first selection of the draft.

Chapter 5

David Robinson graduated from the Naval Academy in 1987 with a degree in mathematics. His first assignment as an officer was to help supervise construction at the Navy's Trident submarine base at Kings Bay in southeastern Georgia.

Robinson quickly realized how sheltered he had been all his life, first at home and then at the Naval Academy. "I was scared to death," he said of his first experience out on his own. Although he was out of school, Robinson got an education into some of the more serious issues of life, such as race relations. His parents had never discussed with him the prejudice they had faced growing up. The fact that Robinson was black had not been a major issue in his life, even though it had sometimes left him in kind of a "no-man's land." He was so used to living among a majority of white students that he was not particularly comfortable around groups of blacks. At the same time he was aware of being the only black student in many of his classes. Yet he remembered very few unpleasant incidents.

In Georgia, though, Robinson saw the gap that separated

When David thought about the high salary he'd be earning playing basketball, the poverty he saw in Georgia haunted him.

black and white. He was especially disturbed at the sight of poor people struggling to survive in their rundown shelters. This especially haunted him because of the enormous amount of money that the Spurs were going to be paying him just to play a game. Robinson had strong religious beliefs, and one of those beliefs was that riches tend to corrupt a person. "It's hard to be a good person if you're rich," Robinson once said. "My biggest fear is that I won't be a good person."

Few people who had met Robinson were concerned about that. "Classy," "respectful," "thoughtful," and "gentlemanly," were the words most often used to describe him. In the words of one admiring coach, "David Robinson has assumed responsibility for his life from day one."

A number of basketball experts, however, worried about Robinson's basketball future. Robinson became so involved in his new life outside of school that he had little time for basketball. The first sign that Robinson might have lost something on his game came in the 1987 Pan American Games. Robinson scored only 14 points a game for a U.S. team that failed to win the gold medal.

Then in March of 1988 Robinson played in an armed forces tournament. A dominating player such as Robinson should have almost guaranteed a win for Navy. Instead an Army squad thumped Robinson's Navy team, 118–71. One observer reported that Robinson was in such poor shape that he could not get down the court three times in a row.

Those who were counting on Robinson to lead the United States to a gold medal in the 1988 Olympics were horrified. Robinson was sent to a crash training camp with his old coaches. He then went to play in Europe on a team of United States Olympic hopefuls. The rust showed. Robinson seemed to have lost some his offensive polish. His attention span wavered. One of his teammates said, "He doesn't act like he's into these games at all."

Robinson began to pull himself together by the end of the tour. In a game against a strong Spanish team, he swiped shots out of the air and swooped to the basket just like his old self. Robinson seemed to be the dream player who would bring Olympic gold to the United States.

Again, though, a coach's dream turned to a nightmare. The U.S. coach was John Thompson from Georgetown University. He was an intimidating leader, nearly as tall as Robinson and much larger. Thompson knew how he wanted things done, and was used to his players following instructions without question.

Unfortunately that was not Robinson's nature. His curiosity kept prodding him to ask why Thompson wanted him to do certain things. "I don't permit people to question me," Thompson insisted.

Robinson refused to back down. "Thompson wanted me to run into a brick wall," Robinson shrugged. "I analyze things."

The relationship between the coach and the center was cool at best. Both Robinson and the team stumbled badly at times in their games. The United States could not even make a serious second-half run at the Soviet Union in their contest. The team, which included such stars as Kansas All-American Danny Manning, had to settle for third place. That was the worst finish ever for an American team in the Olympics. Basketball fans in the United States were outraged. Much of the blame was put on Robinson for his lackluster average of 12.8 points and 6.8 rebounds per game.

Suddenly the Spurs investment did not seem like such a good deal. They had paid the price for Robinson's absence with two horrendous seasons. They had won 52 games and lost 112 with Robinson on active duty. Now, with paid

After his disappointing performance at the Olympics, David Robinson didn't look like such a good investment to the San Antonio Spurs.

attendance dipping below 9,000 per home game, the Spurs were desperate for an instant star. But if the Olympics were any indication, Robinson's skills seemed to have faded already—and his two-year active-duty hitch was only half over. Worse yet, there were doubts that he really had the desire to be a winner. Basketball experts wondered if Robinson was simply too smart and too well-rounded a person to spend so much time on a game like basketball.

Chapter 6

San Antonio coach Larry Brown was determined to keep his new dream player from turning into his worst nightmare. He knew that long losing streaks can dampen anyone's enthusiasm for a game. Rather than let Robinson struggle with a hapless team the way star college center Patrick Ewing had done at New York, Brown brought in some good players. He picked up veteran All-Star forward Terry Cummings from Milwaukee in exchange for two promising young players. Maurice Cheeks came over from Philadelphia to direct the offense. Arizona University star Sean Elliott came via the college draft. Brown even picked up 39-year old center Caldwell Jones to give Robinson some personal instruction in how to play center in the NBA.

For his part Lieutenant David Robinson was pleased to be coming to San Antonio. He liked the idea of starting out with a struggling team and helping to turn them into winners. A shy loner much of his life, he also preferred a smaller city to the pressure of playing in a huge city such as New York. Even in San Antonio, David felt he would be much more comfortable if his parents were around for his first year. Being retired they were not tied to their Washington, D.C. location and were able to join him. To make a move more appealing, David bought them a home in San Antonio.

Both Robinson and Brown knew that the two-year layoff had hurt him. Normally he would have learned and improved during those two years, but instead he lost some of his skill. Even so, his raw talent was obvious. On July 25, 1989, Brown turned his new center loose in an intersquad game against other rookies and free agents. Robinson looked more like the Navy terror of old than the Olympic disappointment. He was the next best thing to having a magnetic force field protecting the basket—he blocked 14 shot attempts. With 31 points and 17 rebounds he showed that he could be a force in the months to come.

During the preseason Robinson found out quickly why pros laugh when they hear basketball described as a noncontact sport. The leaning and shoving and elbowing for position under the basket was fierce. "I expected physical play," Robinson said, shaking his head. "But not this bad." Although he had built up bulging biceps through a weight-lifting program and had boosted his weight to about 235 pounds, Robinson realized that he was not going to overpower pro centers. On the average most NBA centers outweighed him by about 20 pounds. The best he could hope for was to match their strength.

Robinson also realized that he had not yet developed many offensive moves. Nor did he have a favorite shot that he could always count on. He realized that if he wanted to dominate he would have to use his speed and athletic ability.

"Run, run, run!" Robinson thought to himself when he was on the court. He knew that no one his size could stay with him in sprinting up and down the court. He counted on outracing his heavier opponents to the basket for easy layups. When the team was not fast-breaking, he would have to work hard to hold his position against the big bodies. And he would have to use his quickness and athletic skill to get around them.

Robinson's first NBA game was just the kind of headline matchup he did not want. Earvin "Magic" Johnson and the flashy Los Angeles Lakers were coming to San Antonio. But Robinson wasted no time in showing that he could ignore the media attention and stand up to punishment in the lane. In the first quarter he drew three fouls on the Lakers while battling for position.

During the third period the Spurs clung to a narrow lead. Magic Johnson charged into the lane for a layup that would tie the game at 72–72. Robinson ignored Johnson's fakes and stayed with him as he brought the ball to the hoop. Neatly Robinson flicked the ball away. That was as close as the

Under attack from the Lakers, Robinson has learned that an NBA court is no place to be timid.

Robinson outsprints the Lakers for an easy two points.

Lakers would get. With Robinson scoring 23 points and taking 17 rebounds, San Antonio pulled away to win the game 106–98.

After the game, Magic Johnson had news for the Robinson-doubters. "Some rookies are never really rookies," Johnson marveled. "Robinson is one of them."

Over in the Spurs' locker room Robinson accidently demonstrated the wide range of abilities. When asked about his block against Magic, Robinson's thoughtful response was, "My job is to keep the opponent from taking the ball to the hoop with impunity." None of the sports reporters could ever remember hearing a player describe a play in quite that way before. But then none of them had interviewed a pro center who had read a dictionary as a child!

Throughout the season it was obvious that Robinson's mind was a great challenge for a basketball coach. With his love of learning, he eagerly soaked up the teaching of Brown and Caldwell Jones. But occasionally he would tune out his surroundings and wander around the court in a fog. Robinson admitted the problem. There were times when he found himself just watching the action around him, as if he were not really a part of it.

Wisely Brown did not take it as a personal insult to his coaching. He knew that Robinson was just different from other players. Although he prodded his center to keep focused, he let Robinson take control of his own career. "David's got to decide how badly he wants it," Brown said.

Some critics thought Robinson's wide range of interests and hobbies blocked his path to greatness. But the rookie just brushed off those comments. "Funny," he said, "most of the time they want athletes to take a little more interest in the rest of life." Most fans admired Robinson for sticking to his belief that sports are not the most important thing in life; that there is more to life than winning and losing.

No matter what anyone said Robinson's thirst for learning was never satisfied. He bought a baby grand piano for his room so that he could play his classical music. Since that was too big to take with him on road trips, he packed an electronic keyboard. Teammate Terry Cummings turned out to have a similar interest in music. The two of them enjoyed spending time together, playing and singing songs that they had composed. Robinson also brought along video games and logic books to fill the time on long road trips. If Robinson was having trouble concentrating on the game, few NBA opponents noticed. With Robinson's long left hand looming over them, ready to block their shots, they had their own trouble concentrating. The Golden State Warriors were one team that caught the full force of the rookie's concentration.

Teammate Terry Cummings was in tune with Robinson both on and off the court.

Bounding and soaring across the court like some fantasy avenger, Robinson scored 41 points, blocked 5 shots, and collected 17 rebounds in the game.

There were also certain players on whom Robinson had no trouble focusing. Ever since he had reported to camp, experts had compared him to the reigning "towers of power" in the NBA, Hakeem Olajuwon of Houston and Patrick Ewing of New York. Olajuwon was a Nigerian who, like Robinson, did not begin playing basketball until later in life. But quickness, strength, and athletic skill had made him the NBA's best center. Olajuwon was the defending NBA rebounding champ and had finished tenth in the league in scoring the previous year.

The stronger, more ferocious Ewing was Olajuwon's main competition for the top spot. Ewing, a Jamaican who moved to the United States at the age of 11, had recently perfected a deadly selection of offensive moves to go with his already tough defense.

If David Robinson wanted to be the best, these were the men he would have to pass. Both Olajuwon and Ewing had read about Robinson and were determined to prove that they were still the kings of the hill.

Fans looked forward to see how the rookie would fare in his first test against these giants. Two months into the season, Robinson got his chance. On December 14, 1989, Olajuwon and the Houston Rockets came to San Antonio. The two big men battled tirelessly, constantly forcing the other away from his favorite shots. Although Olajuwon won the rebounding battle, Robinson outscored him by 19 to 15. The Spurs' center held his more experienced rival to a frustrating 5 out of 17 shots from the field.

When congratulated on battling Houston's star to a draw,

Robinson slips past All-Pro rival Hakeem Olajuwon for the slam.

Robinson showed a flash of competitive fire. "I don't want to be neutral. I want to dominate."

In January of 1990, Robinson faced back-to-back road games against Boston's steady veteran Robert Parish, and New York's Ewing. First the rookie outscored Parish by 18 to 11 as San Antonio broke a 20-game losing streak at the Boston Garden.

Two nights later, Robinson took on Ewing and the Knicks at Madison Square Garden. Eager to defend his turf against this new rival, Ewing played fiercely. The rookie Robinson was badgered into making six turnovers. But he stood his ground against the 255-pound Ewing. Twice he blocked Ewing's shots, once on a dunk attempt. Before long it was Ewing who was forced to the bench with foul trouble.

Late in the game Ewing staked out a position near the free throw line. He backed into Robinson so hard that David stumbled ten feet backward. New York's Gerald Wilkens saw Ewing standing wide open and threw a pass to him. Robinson recovered so quickly that he snatched the pass on the run to start a fast break. New York won the game by 107-101, but Robinson outscored a major rival for the third straight time. He scored 27 points while holding Ewing to 18. That total was 10 points below the Knick star's average.

Although he had plenty of help from Cummings, Cheeks, and Elliott, Robinson was given most of the credit for leading San Antonio to the most dramatic about-face in NBA history. The Spurs, who had finished a woeful 21–61 the previous season, came alive to win 56 and lose only 26 in 1989–90. Robinson finished second in the NBA to Olajuwon in rebounding with a 12.0 average, third in blocks (3.8 average), and tenth in scoring (24.3 points per game). With that kind of performance Robinson won every vote in the balloting for NBA rookie of the year.

Robinson pulls down a rebound against the NBA champion Detroit Pistons.

San Antonio moved on to the playoffs—an unfamiliar experience for the Spurs. They roared through the first round, sweeping the Denver Nuggets in a three-game series. Robinson stepped up his effort a notch from his fine regular season. He averaged more than 28 points and 13 rebounds against the Nuggets.

The ease of their win left the Spurs unprepared for a more typical playoff series against Portland. The Trailblazers were considered by some to be the best collection of athletes in the NBA. They danced all over the Spurs in the first game of their seven-game set. Robinson played in a fog, making only 3 of 11 shots. He finished the game with just 9 points and 9 rebounds.

The poor effort woke him up. Robinson charged into game number two with such enthusiasm that the normally polite, mild-mannered center was whistled for a technical foul. He slammed home 31 points, but it was not enough to beat Portland.

Back at their own HemisFair Arena, the Spurs regrouped. Robinson intimidated the visitors with 8 blocked shots and 28 points as the Spurs won game three. He then played a quieter role as San Antonio blew out their rivals to win game four.

Back in Portland for game five, Robinson defended his basket skillfully. He scored 27 points and pulled down 15 rebounds to keep his team in the game. But when he fouled out late in the game, San Antonio's hopes for an upset were dashed. With their star center on the bench the Spurs finally fell to a heartbreaking 138–132 double-overtime loss.

Robinson played his normal game, 24 points, 13 rebounds, as the Spurs won game six easily. Now the series had come down to one final game on Portland's home court.

Robinson opened the crucial game with a horrible shooting exhibition. Three of his shots were blocked by

Passing up a chance for a shot, Robinson looks to pass to an open teammate.

Portland's high-flying forwards. Bothered by Portland's 7-foot, 270-pound Kevin Duckworth, Robinson missed 10 of his first 11 shooting attempts. All he could do was work hard on his rebounding and defense until he regained his shooting touch.

The big center started connecting in the second half as San Antonio rallied past the Trailblazers. The Spurs took a 97–90 lead with two and a half minutes to go in the game, and seemed on their way to the conference semifinals. But Portland put on a furious final burst to send yet another game into overtime. Robinson's 20 points and 16 rebounds were not enough to stop the Trailblazers. The Portland team wrapped up a thrilling postseason series with a 108–105 win.

Robinson's exciting first year as a pro was over. Experts wondered if Robinson would be different now that he knew how good he could good be. Would he get hooked on basketball and back away from his other interests?

But Robinson was not about to put those kinds of limits on himself. When he reported to the Spurs' training camp for the 1990–91 season, he was carrying a new toy. He had become fascinated with the music of the saxophone and was determined to teach himself how to play.

Chapter 7

After their great success the previous season, the young Spurs team was expected to challenge for the NBA title in 1990–91. Sure enough they shot off to a fast start and raced to the top of the Midwest Division. With a year's experience behind him Robinson felt more comfortable taking the court against the NBA giants. He scored more, rebounded more, and blocked more shots than he had during his first season.

Everything seemed to be going his way off-court as well as on-court. Other than a frustrated coach or two that he had left in his wake, there was hardly a person in the world who had a bad word to say about him. People admired Robinson's respectful manners, his open, honest communication, and the way he honored his commitment to the Navy. Robinson tried to use his wealth to help others. He also treated fans well. Once he stopped to pump gasoline at a self-service station in San Antonio. He was soon surrounded by fans who recognized him. Robinson patiently stood in the rain signing autographs for the fans.

Robinson's glowing reputation was enhanced by a shoe

company. They brought out a series of popular "Mr. Robinson's Neighborhood" ads. Robinson's popularity grew so quickly that he won more All-Star votes from the fans than any other Western Conference player in the 1990–91 balloting—including Magic Johnson.

Robinson enjoyed living in San Antonio. He was not the kind of person who went out partying or looking for excitement. His idea of a good time was the same as it had always been. "Learning stuff" was what he most enjoyed doing, and he preferred quiet activities at home. Robinson admitted that most people probably would think he was boring to live around. "But I wouldn't trade places with anyone," he said. "I'm having the best time in the world."

A season that started out so promising, however, soon began to go sour. The Spurs were hobbled by a series of injuries to key players. Rod Strickland, the young point guard who had replaced Maurice Cheeks, was forced out of action for several weeks because of injuries. Then Terry Cummings joined him on the injured list.

With those players out of the lineup, Robinson was called upon to provide more scoring punch. That was when some of the flaws in Robinson's game began to show. Despite his high scoring average, Robinson still had not perfected a trademark offensive move. When the Spurs passed the ball to Robinson in the low post, he did not always know what to do with it. Although he owned a soft, left-handed jump shot, he had trouble getting himself into position to use it. Only a few of his points came from shots off of set plays. During a game against the Denver Nuggets, for instance, Robinson scored 24 of his 31 points on slam dunks.

"I don't have all the basics down yet," Robinson admitted. Coach Brown had to agree. "When I see Ewing or Olajuwon play, David isn't there yet," he said.

The people's choice as the Western Conference All-Star center, Robinson shoots
over Eastern Conference All-Star Charles Barkley.

Just after the Spurs were hit with injuries, events halfway around the globe brought Robinson face to face with the grim side of life. On January 16, 1991, Robinson was sitting in the Spurs dressing room before a game with the Dallas Mavericks when word came of war with Iraq in the Persian Gulf. Upon hearing reports of the first bombing runs, "my stomach just dropped," Robinson said. Many of his Naval Academy classmates and friends were sailing the ships and flying bombing missions. Were it not for a fluke of nature that caused him to grow six inches after high school graduation, Robinson would probably have been among them.

Robinson sat glued to the television set in the locker room until it was time to go out for the game. San Antonio won the contest by a score of 100–94, but Robinson's heart was not in it. "The war makes the significance of this game very small. I've only been in mock war situations and those were not fun

Injuries to teammates in 1990-91 forced Robinson to look for a way to score, as he does here against the Lakers' Vlade Divac.

at all. They give you a real sense of the reality of war. It's a sobering experience."

During the fighting the media were looking for unique angles on war coverage. Robinson was a lieutenant in the Naval Select Reserve, and so he was often approached as a celebrity expert on war. But he avoided commenting on the fighting. "I didn't feel like I was really qualified to be talking about it."

The turmoil of the war affected Robinson's play, according to his coaches. He insisted that he blocked it out of his mind while on the court, but he lacked his usual aggressiveness. The Spurs wasted a number of huge leads in games during that period, winning only 10 of 19 games.

By the time the fighting ended in March, and Cummings and Strickland returned to the lineup, the Spurs had fallen back into a wild scramble for the division lead. The Utah Jazz

Robinson concentrates on a free throw.

and Olajuwon's Houston Rockets both caught the stumbling Spurs late in the season. It was time for David to prove that the area around the basket really was "Mr. Robinson's Neighborhood."

In the last few weeks of the season, Robinson stalked opposing players with the quickness and cunning he had shown earlier in the season. Those careless enough to challenge Robinson could suffer their choice of humiliations. Robinson could either strip the ball from them before they got their shot off, or leap high to block the shot if they did get it off. On two occasions he swatted away 11 shots in a single game.

There was no way for a team to play a normal game when Robinson was terrorizing the court. In the words of Charlotte Hornets Coach Matt Goukas, "He distorts your whole game." Robinson distorted enough games so that the Spurs were able to edge out Houston in the last game of the season to win the Midwest crown.

Robinson improved in every area of his game during his second season. With Olajuwon injured for part of the year, Robinson easily won the NBA rebounding title with an average of 13 per game. He boosted his scoring average to 25.6, the ninth best mark in the NBA. He also blocked more shots than anyone else in the league.

Robinson was the main reason that San Antonio entered the playoffs as one of the favorites to contend for the NBA championship. The Spurs' first round opponent, Golden State, appeared to be an easy victim. The Warriors had the second worst record among Western Conference playoff teams. They had no center who could come close to matching Robinson.

It was not a good year for dominating centers, though. First Patrick Ewing and the Knicks were blown out by the

Bulls in the first round. Then Olajuwon and the Rockets were swept by the Lakers in their first round series.

Golden State did not even try to match up against Robinson and the Spurs. Instead they used a coaching gimmick. They went with a small, quick lineup, often using four guards on the court at one time. Robinson played well as the teams split the first two games of the series. In the first three games, he averaged more than 28 points and 13 rebounds. But after a while he began to look like a man trying to catch squirrels. The smaller Golden State team shocked the Spurs by taking the series three games to one.

Robinson was deeply disappointed by the early exit from the playoffs. "This is tough," he said to reporters afterward. "I don't feel like I fulfilled my responsibilities." As Robinson had shown in the Navy, duty was important to him. He had

Robinson defends the basket against a drive by Golden State's Mitch Richmond in play-off action.

every intention of giving the Spurs and their fans their money's worth.

But as coaches were beginning to understand, he could only do that by being himself. He could not pretend that basketball was his whole life. "What good is it being the greatest basketball player if you're the most miserable?" Robinson once asked.

Many people are convinced that Robinson is close to being the greatest just as he is. Robinson leaped past Ewing and Olajuwon to win the sportswriters' vote as the NBA's top center in 1991. In a computerized rating of basketball players published by *The Sporting News* in 1991, Robinson ranked with Michael Jordan as the two top players in the NBA.

He has accomplished all this despite still being relatively new at the game. Furthermore, he has vowed to get better. "Soon I'm going to know how to do all those basic things, and I'm going to be better off," Robinson said during the 1990–91 season.

That is what worries his NBA opponents. After hearing so much talk about Robinson's lack of experience, New Jersey Net guard Mookie Blaylock could only mutter. "If he's still learning the game, I'd hate to see him when he knows it stone cold."

Career Statistics

College

Year	Team	GP	FG%	REB	PTS	AVG
1983-84	U.S. Naval Academy	28	.623	111	214	7.6
1984-85	U.S. Naval Academy	32	.644	370	756	23.6
1985-86	U.S. Naval Academy	35	.607	455	796	22.7
1986-87	U.S. Naval Academy	32	.591	378	903	28.2
	TOTAL	127	.613	1314	2669	21.0

NBA

Year	Team	GP	FG%	REB	AST	STL	BLK	PTS	AVG
1989-90	San Antonio	82	.531	983	164	138	319	1993	24.3
1990-91	San Antonio	82	.552	1063	208	127	320	2101	25.6
	TOTAL	164	.542	2046	372	265	639	4094	25.0

Index

WAYNE-WESTLAND LIBRARY